THE BILLION DOLLAR
Baby

The incredible true story
of a miracle baby who
survived the greatest odds

Calvin Ward

THE BILLION DOLLAR

The incredible true story
of a miracle baby who
survived the greatest odds

Calvin Ward

T&J PUBLISHERS

A SMALL INDEPENDENT PUBLISHER WITH A BIG VOICE

Printed in the United States of America by
T&J Publishers (Atlanta, GA.)
www.TandJPublishers.com

All Bible verses are from the King James Version (KJV) and the New American Standard Bible (NASB)

Cover design by Timothy Flemming, Jr.
(T&J Publishers)

Book format and layout by Timothy Flemming, Jr.
(T&J Publishers)

ISBN: 978-0-9994121-6-9

To contact the author, go to:

Calvinward2002@yahoo.com
www.NewLifeAtHopkins.com
Facebook: Bishop Calvin D. Ward
Facebook: Newlifeathopkins

ACKNOWLEDGEMENTS

First, I would like to dedicate this book to my God: the Father, the Son, and the Holy Spirit. Without God, I would not have made it. He is my joy, my peace, and my strength.

I sincerely thank my mother Susanne Ward Jones for being a great mom and for never giving up on me.

I want to thank my dad Willie Calvin Jones for teaching me to not judge people based on their relationship with others and not allowing time to pass before forgiving people.

I want to thank my brother Keith Jones for always being there to protect me when others tried to take advantage of me.

I would to thank Thelma "Ma" Ward, my rock, the one who told me that I can do anything in life. Thanks for never giving up on me. I can still hear your voice in my ear, saying, "Never give up regardless of who quites believing in you."

I want to the my amazing wife Keiyawna Ward for excepting me for who I am and loving me in-spite of my disabilities. Thank you for teaching me that marriage is a blessing as long as you put God first, family second, passion third, and finances last.

I would like to thank my awesome family: my girls

Kahleighya, Kemia, and Kaela for making me feel like the best dad in the world.

Lastly, I would like to thank my church family for your prayers and support as well as my friends. May God bless you richly.

"For I know the plans I have for you, says the LORD, They are plans for good and not for disaster, to give you a future and hope." - Jeremiah 29:11, New American Standard Bible (NASB)

TABLE OF CONTENTS

INTRODUCTON

THIS BOOK IS ENTITLED "THE BILLION DOLLAR Baby" because that is how costly my surgical procedures were just to keep me alive as a child. My condition is rare - very rare. I am one of the few humans on the planet born with my rare condition. I am as of today the only person born in the United States of America with my condition. I am one of the only ones who has been born with my rare condition and has lived to tell about it. This is my story, the testimony of a man born with a condition not many people in this world has. You're getting ready to dive into the life of a baby it took a billion dollars just to keep alive, one who is as rare as the condition he has. Yes, I am rare. How so? Because people who haven't even faced the type of hardship, ridicule, and persecution that I've faced still find it difficult to smile; and yet, I smile...through it all. The joy in my soul is unusual, is rare, but it is not without cause. It is because of my walk with God that I can smile while living with three rare disabilities.

There is one Bible verse that serves as a guiding light for my life, which I live by daily. It is found in Luke

4:18-19. It reads,

> "For the Spirit of the Lord is upon me, because he
> hath anointed me to preach the gospel to the poor;
> he hath sent me to heal the brokenhearted, to preach
> deliverance to the captives, and recovering of sight
> to the blind, to set a liberty them that are bruised.
> To preach the acceptable year of the Lord."

This reminds me that every day of my life, I have a purpose
to fulfill. There is a reason behind every pain, every prob-
lem, and every condition. No one is an accident. It's time to
discover the reason you were born and how God intends
to use your life for His glory.

Part 1
The Purpose

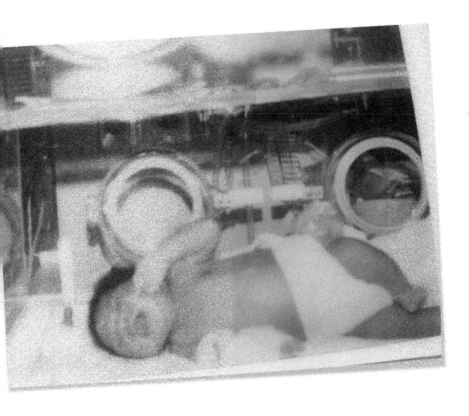

CHAPTER 1

The Birth of The Billion-Dollar Baby

O N OCTOBER 15, 1979, IN ATLANTA GEORGIA, Susanne Ward and Willie Calvin Jones, Jr. found themselves rushing to Grady Hospital to give birth to me. It was an exciting time for them. I was getting ready to enter into the world. I'm Susanne's firstborn child. For Willie (also known as "Jr."), I was his third child. He already had a daughter and a son.

Oh, the joy on Susanne's face. She came from a large family. She was the last of fourteen children: ten girls and four boys. Her parents were Samuel and Thelma Ward. Thelma, better known as "Ma," was the rock of the Ward family. Jr. who was the oldest of his siblings (of the Jones family) was on his way to the NBA straight out of high school until he started having kids.

Everyone was full of joy and excitement until Dr. Ricketts walked out of the delivery room. His facial expression and the tone of his voice revealed to the family that there was a problem. "What's wrong with my baby!" Susanne screamed. "What's wrong! What's wrong with my baby!" Ma, sitting next to Susanne's side, then asked,

"What's going on, baby? Tell me! Tell me right now!"

Dr. Ricketts, with a sense of dread in his eyes, looked at the family and said, "Out of all of my years of practicing medicine and being the top Physician at Emory, your son Calvin has one of the rarest cases of abnormalities that myself or my team has encountered. What your son Calvin has is called Imperforate Anus with a post-pull through Rectal Agenesis, Colostomy Retropratate Fistula Repair. His second clinical indication is Congenital Genitourinary Abnormalities, Neurogenic Bladder, and a Descended Bladder. His third disability is an enlarged kidney with Hydronephrosis with Cortical Thinning. Calvin will have to wear a colostomy bag. Also, his bowels don't have movements. If he lives in the years to come, we will create an anus for him; but the problem could be there may not be any nerves and feeling in his anus, which can cause fecal insanities for your child. I'm sorry Ms. Ward and Mr. Jones and the Jones and Ward families. Your youngest grandchild is not expected to live past two to three hours."

"What are you saying, Doctor Ricketts?!" asked Ma. "Please speak plainly to us! What's going on?! What do you mean, 'Your son, my grandson, is sick unto death'?" Doctor Ricketts then informed the family,

"Calvin's kidneys, bowels, and bladder are all deformed, and the dysfunctional one is larger than the other, which causes him to be unable to urinate on his own, and he has no anus to have bowel movements. There's no way for him to use the restroom on his own. His kidney's deformity will cause him to have a kidney infection for the rest of his life if he continues to live. I'm sorry. He will never be like other kids. He will never be normal. It will take a miracle to reconstruct his body just so that he could live with his disabilities."

Upon hearing this news, Susanne busted into tears. She began crying out to God, asking, "God, why?!!" At that moment, Jr. got upset and began ranting,

"Calvin is not my child! He's retarded, disable, and deformed! Nothing is wrong with my other two children! He can't be my child!" Meanwhile, Ma calmly began to pray:

"Lord, you make no mistakes; so, work a miracle right now. God, you have plans for Calvin. You want him to live and not die." She just prayed earnestly to God. She then called Bishop Willis Paden who was the bishop of her church at the time. She asked him to pray for me, for God to work a miracle in my life. She explained to Bishop Paden that the doctor announced that I wasn't going to live very long, but that she believed in the miracle-working power of God to bring a healing into my life. Bishop Paden, along with other ministers and church members, began praying for my healing. They were calling out my name, asking God to let me live, asking God to perform a miracle in my body. It was amazing! There were hundreds of Believers praying and fasting for God to perform a miracle in my life.

Later, Dr. Ricketts approached the families and told

them, "I'm going to perform a surgery that has never been tried before in the United States. Your child will surely die if we do nothing. So let's try, even if it's an experiment." This experimental surgery cost millions of dollars. It was grueling, daring, challenging, but the hand of God was guiding his hands. Dr. Ricketts succeeded in creating me an anus. He could then safely remove the colostomy bag. He reconstructed my kidneys. "Susanne and Willie, there are no promises, but I will assure you that we will do our very best," Dr. Ricketts assured my parents.

The next few years was like watching paint dry. No one knew how things would turn out. Over the next five years of my life after that surgery, I lived in and out of the hospital. I experienced cantharis six to ten times a day. I suffered from urinary tract infection. My bowels were inconsistent every day, all day. I had no feeling in my anus. One of my kidneys worked at only twenty percent; the other one was overworked. My right bladder only functioned at thirty percent; the left bladder barely functioned at all. There was a specially made enema bag designed just for me; it was shipped to the US from Canada to be tested on me. I had nothing to lose, but everything to gain at this point. Ultimately, God was in control. The proof of this is the fact that I'm alive today. Yes, I live with certain disabilities, but for a child who was given only a few hours to live upon birth, I'd say I'm a miracle in the flesh. Problems everyday but alive never normal, but alive. My body not only experienced a miracle, but my family did as well. The Wards and the Jones didn't necessarily see eye to eye. They didn't like each other and got along very much. But my condition brought them together like never before. That, too, was a miracle. It's interesting how God has a way of using one situation to produce healings and miracles in so many areas of our lives. When God has a purpose for your life, there is nothing that can stop His plans. But know that your purpose in life will only be brought to pass through a process. And it would be over the next few years of my life that I would discover God's purpose and plan for my life and experience the process that one must go through to step into their divine destiny. Yes, we'll experience some positives and negatives during this process, but we must always remember that all things work together for the good of them that love God and are called according to His purpose. Don't complain. Thank God for the process. It will all be worth it in the end as you'll discover through my story.

THE BILLION DOLLAR BABY

CHAPTER 2

The Lost Years

AFTER FIVE YEARS OF LIVING IN THE HOSPITAL - missing Headstart, preschool, kindergarten, and first grade - I was finally able to go home, I was finally allowed to running around at grandmother's (Ma's) house and meet the rest of my family. I was trying to fit in, not knowing what was going on with my health. All I heard was "Don't touch him right there! Stop running, Calvin! Sit down! Don't jump! Don't fall!" I was starting to think that something is wrong with everyone. It was as if everyone else were keeping a secret from me. I didn't know it then that I had a sickness, a disability. But eventually, I made that discovery. One day, I smelled an odor that was very unpleasant. When the odor seeped out into the air, I heard everyone asking, "Who boo-booed?" Someone then screamed,

"It's Calvin! He stinks!" That's when it hit me. That's when I sensed that something was wrong with me. You see, I didn't feel my bowels leaking out of my body. I had a bowel movement on myself without realizing it. At first, I didn't understand why kids and even my family members would say such hurtful things about me. I would hear people say things to and about me like "Stinky boy! Doo-doo Boy!" It was stressful being outside in the scorching heat and wondering why flies would be following me and hearing all of the mean jokes about me. That was just the beginning of my troubles. Of course, the most hurtful words came from my close family members.

I remember starting school. I was going to Collier Elementary School. My first grade my teacher Mrs. Hunter had read and understood my history, she knew my disabilities, but she still wasn't fully prepared for the reality of my situation, and neither were my peers. It happen again: I had a bowel movement on myself. The kids went crazy. I smelled like a walking corpse. Ms. Hunter sprayed three cans of air fresher and placed a temporary air freshener under her nose. She then removed my desk outside of the classroom so that I would be isolated from the rest of the class. Truthfully, I wasn't ready for this chapter in my life. I never imagined that kids could be so mean. I never imagined that a teacher could be so misunderstanding; this was the worst feeling in the world, and it was starting to affect my education and my self-esteem. I found myself being lonely and alone a lot. To a degree, being alone felt better than being picked on all of the time by my classmates, but it still carried a lot of pain.

After this experience, I felt as if couldn't return to school. The school work was easy, but my body was in horrible shape. Mrs. Hunter couldn't take it. My classmates couldn't take it. After all of the physical and emotional pain I experienced and the repeated hospital visits, I began to feel like I could no longer take it. That day, after I got home from school, I had another bowel movement on myself. My mother did not know what to do with me. She couldn't fully understand why this was happening to her child. My dad was still in a state of denial. He couldn't accept the fact that his child was disabled. After having another bowel movement on myself, my dad - who was a big man, standing at 6'4 - picked me up, took his weightlifting belt, and beat me like I stole something. He thought I was using the restroom on myself on purpose and that I simply refused to go to the restroom. He refused to accept the fact that I was disabled and had no control over my bowels. It seemed difficult to find love from my family and my friends. It seemed as if even the teachers, who I thought would have been a little more professional and understanding regarding my condition, were willing to help me. My disability truly put me in a lonely place.

While my dad was beating me, he kept yelling, "He's not my child!!" My mom was screaming back at him,

"He can't help it!!!" I didn't understand what I did wrong in that moment - why my father was so angry with me. I wanted to move to a safe environment, so I told my mother I wanted to go home to my grandma's house. Mom and dad were experiencing marital problems anyway. At the time, I didn't know that my dad had other kids: Willie and Valetta. My mother, at twenty-five years old, wanted me home with her, but with a failing marriage, two of her own biological children, and two step children to deal with, my disability was stressing her out. All I could think about was hearing my dad holler, "I didn't create a disable child!" All I could remember myself saying was,

"I'm sorry! I didn't mean to do it, daddy! I'm sorry!" Mom was crying. My brother was crying. All I cared about was going to Ma's house. I believe the reality of the situation finally sunk into my mother's head: that me living in Atlanta with my father was not the best thing for me. So, my mother let me live with my grandma. For years, I'd visit my parents in their apartments in Either Ridge Courts and Bank Head Court. But my safe haven was located across the Chattahoochee River in Cobb County, Georgia.

Part 2
The Process

Chapter 3

The Most Hated Years

I TRANSFERRED FROM AN ALL-BLACK SCHOOL TO AN all-white school thinking things would be different, but they weren't. I had hoped that the kids at this school wouldn't be so mean and harsh towards me. I remember stepping into my first-grade class and seeing the teacher, Miss Riggins - she had the same look on her face that Mrs. Hunter did. That was a bad sign. Furthermore, as expected, I had a bowel movement on myself while in class. And, yes, as you'd imagine, my classmates went crazy. At that moment, I realized that I didn't have a racial problem, I had a Calvin-problem. These kids were the same as the ones at the previous school I transferred from; this was just more of the same.

I couldn't catheterize myself six to eight times daily. I had bowel movements on myself multiple times throughout the day while in school, at home, at church, in the car, at the park - every day, all times a day. I felt helpless. No one was on my side except for Ma, my mother, and my brother Keith. I hated going to school. I hate it trying to fit in when no one wanted to be around me. For the first time, a teacher named Ms. Cutler threw understood me. She threw her arms around me and said, "Calvin, everything is going to be alright." I didn't know whether to believe her or not, but it sure felt good just to know that someone outside of my small circle cared about me rather than judged and criticized me for something I couldn't control. Ms. Cutler protected me all the way through elementary school, but no one warned me about middle school. That would be a life-changing experience for me. My first week in middle school was horrible; it was all about who had the best shoes, the best clothes, the best hair, jewelry, etc. Of course, I was trying to fit in, but my disability wouldn't let that happen. While sitting in class, it happened again: I had a bowel movement on myself. This time, it wasn't one who gave me that funny look, it was five to eight teachers; it wasn't one classroom either, it was all of the classrooms I had to go to; this occurred my entire time in middle school - the sixth through eighth grade. I can't begin to express how bad things got fully. I had no friends and no one to talk to; they didn't understand, they didn't even know I had a disability. I wanted to tell my peers so badly about my disability, but I was afraid to because I felt the need to fit in so badly. I remember this girl, Tamika Jones; she was singing one of Atlanta's hit songs "Doo-Doo Brown". All of my peers were singing it along with her. I felt so humiliated. All I could think of was going home, jumping into the bed, going to sleep and never waking up again. I wanted to die. I began to think to myself, "Heaven has to be better than this." My teachers came together and tried to figure out ways to help me without making a scene every time I had an accident. There wasn't a single incident in which wasn't severely embarrassed. Miss Williams, a teacher from my middle school, didn't think that I should be in the same school with her and the other students. She let it be known to the principal, Missy Elliott. Whenever I'd walk down the hall, she would look at me like I had leprosy or AIDs. She would stay as far away from me as she could. Being the person that I am, I would try to be kind and speak to her, but those big white eyes of hers would just stretch wide whenever I got near her, and she would tense up, her face squinting, and she'd just keep walking as if ignoring me. I began to think that she was on a mission to get me suspended or expelled from school.

My absolute worst day in middle school was when I messed all over myself in class. I then went to the bathroom - my clothes were all damaged from my bowels. Usually, whenever this would happen, I'd just wash my clothes out in the bathroom and then everything would be alright. But this time, when I washed my clothes in the sink, the smell wouldn't go away. When I went back to the classroom, my underwear was still damp. In my mind, I was clean because the load in my underwear was gone, but that wasn't the case. When I walked into the classroom, my classmates were appalled; they were putting their fingers up to their noses and frowning in disgust. It smelled like a newborn baby had just dropped a load in their pants, only that I wasn't a newborn; I was twelve years old. I stunk up the whole room. Picture a room full of sixth graders all screaming out of disgust while looking at you. I felt like sinking through the floor. To make things worst, they began singing what had seemingly become my theme song around the school: "Doo-Doo Brown". My mind immediately went blank. I just left the room and called my mom. All I wanted to do was get away. I wanted to be all by myself. I didn't want a hug; I didn't want anyone comforting me; I just wanted to be alone. My teacher sent me to the principal's office. The principal, Miss Elliot, had this expression on her face as if I had committed a crime. She yelled at me for causing such a disturbance in class. At that time, my teacher was Mr. Newsome. He tried to take up for me, reminding the principal that I couldn't control my bowels, but also present was Miss Williams. Oh, she was so happy to get her day in court finally. She was the lawyer, and Miss Elliott was the judge. I was the criminal who was on trial. They took turns viciously going at me. I remember hearing Miss Williams' voice. She was saying, "I told you that I would get him. I told you." I noticed the look on Miss Elliot's face when the deliberations were through. That was it. I was through. I knew this was the last straw. Miss Elliot expelled me from school. I was officially out of my teachers' hair and away from the student body. Miss Elliot had finally gotten rid of the problem that stunk up the school.

When I went home, I strongly thought about what had just happened to me. Expelled?!! I'd never even been in detention nor ISS (in school suspension). I'd never been in any trouble. And now, I've been expelled. I didn't get into a fight, bring drugs to school, bring a weapon to school, or did anything else of the kind; I simply possessed a disability (or set of disabilities actually) that I had no control over. After going to the doctor's office, I was granted with a letter officially stating that no teacher, student, principal, counselor, or anyone else could deny me the right to go to the restroom and spend as much time as I needed. I was reinstated back in school. When I was allowed back in school, you should have seen the look on Miss Elliot's face. She couldn't believe I was back in her school. I didn't harbor any bad feelings in my heart towards her nor Miss Williams. Unfortunately, for Miss Elliot, she ended up experiencing a serious car accident, one that in a sense left her disabled. She ended up breaking her neck and was never allowed to return to the school to work. Her doctor informed her that one accident - one hit, one fall, etc. - would leave her paralyzed for life. Of course, I did think about it; it did seem like a case of irony or even poetic justice: she attacked me because of my disability, and now she has an even more crippling disability of her own. Whatever the case, one thing became apparent to me and those around me: be careful how you treat others. Put another way: What goes around, comes around. After this, an overwhelming sense that there was something supernatural guiding my life rested upon me. I began to feel as if, although rejected by others, someone big - real big - was on my side, looking out for me. At that point, a type of confidence and sense of belonging began to emerge within me. After that, I decided that it was time out with trying to fit in; it was now time to stand out.

CHAPTER 4

Created To Stand Out, Not Fit In

I FELT LIKE I HAD NO ONE THAT I COULD TURN TO, TALK to, and lean on during my ordeal. I had a mind full of questions, but no answers. All I could do was ask God, "Why me?" Many times, I asked God to take my life so that my pain and suffering would come to an end.

I was in the swing of my daily routine: I had to take my medicine; I had catheterize myself (catherization is when you put a tube up your penis and into your bladder so that it can drain the urine out of your system to prevent bacteria from causing a urinary tract infection). I had to do this six to eight times a day. I had to deal with the constant issue of having bowel movements on myself and people criticizing me. It seemed as if my life at this time had come to a standstill. I was stuck in my daily routine. From the age of five to the age of eighteen, I spent at least a week, sometimes two weeks, in the hospital for urinary tract infections. I became tired of my daily routine. I wanted to live like a normal person. I then decided to do something I should not have done: I stopped taking my medicine and following my doctor's instructions, and within one day I almost died. There was so much blood in my urine that it looked like red grapefruit juice. My urine smelled like four-day-old ammonia. My body was in pain from my head to my toes. I crawled into my bed, and I cried. I was fine as long as no one touched me. Even the slightest touch sent pain coursing through my body like a sharp knife piercing through me. I wanted to die. I asked God to please take the pain away. I even asked Him to take my life. One of my aunts came down the stairs into my room. She was adamant that I needed to go to the hospital. I begged her just to let me lie in bed and die, but she refused. She wouldn't let me give up. I had to crawl up the stairs and to the car so that she could take me to the hospital. It was only the grace of God that allowed me to make it to the car and to the hospital in time. My kidney was on the verge of shutting down. The doctors had to put an IV in my arm and flood my body with antibiotics. It took nearly two weeks for me to become healthy again.

Truthfully, I can't say that I regretted my reckless actions that almost cost me my life. I didn't regret my actions. I wished I would have died. And while going through that near-death experience, I didn't have a supernatural experience. There was no white light, nor did I see any angels. I didn't hear the audible voice of God in my ear. I didn't experience any of that. But what I did experience was God's grace keeping me alive. God wouldn't allow me to die. I didn't know then why God kept me alive. I did not understand why he allowed me to live, but I did make a vow that by the age of eighteen I wasn't going to have to take any more medications nor catheterize myself. I vowed never to spend another day in the hospital if possible. If I got another urinary tract infection, it wasn't going to be because I wanted to kill myself. I decided to live because of a statement made to me by a very special person who reminded me that this world can become better because of me and that my family and loved ones truly did need me. They reminded me that I couldn't be all that God created me to be if I didn't take care of my health; they reminded me that if I gave up on life, I'd never get to experience all that God called me to in life.

I began to find my way. I continued to play ball and stay in the church. When playing sports and being in church, I felt a sense of peace, I felt loved and accepted, and I felt like I had a sense of power and control. I could never be what others wanted me to be. I accepted the fact that I was supposed to be what God wanted me to be. I accepted my gifts and my calling. God gave me a gift of leadership, a gift to preach His Word, and the gift to sing; He also gifted me in sports to play ball. I accepted who I am and what God called me to be and decided to stop trying to fit into everyone else's cliques. People knew I had several disabilities, but they also knew I was gifted in many ways. I find it interesting that when people love you for your gifts, they'll put up with your condition.

At this point in my life, I had gained a wealth of knowledge through life's experiences. By the age of twelve,

I was in the ministry, preaching like someone who had lived much longer than I. I would preach the Gospel in the schools to the same individuals that talked about me. I would dress up as a preacher and minister to teachers, students, athletes, and anyone else that would listen. I remember one incident I had during an important ballgame. No, I didn't have a bowel movement on myself - I had given myself an enema beforehand, but I put too much water in my system during the process. One of the coaches I respected and admired revealed his true feelings about me. He was telling all of the kids in the program about the time I crapped all over myself during a football game. All of the kids started laughing at me; the coach was laughing with them. I asked him if he had been aware all of that time that I had a disability. He said yes, but that didn't stop him from making fun of my situation. That truly hurt me because it reminded me of the time when I first came only to be laughed at by my family and friends.

I learned to deal with my emotions of hurt, pain, anger, and even bitterness over the things people said and did to me by praying to God and talking to Him about how I felt. At times, I felt like the woman with the issue of blood in Luke 8:43-48. There weren't many people that didn't know my situation. I hated elementary school and middle school. But my experiences taught me how to treat people; they taught me how to have compassion for others. In what I would deem my hated years, I was developing the type of character necessary to touch and heal the lives of others. Yes, it was a painful process, but it was well worth it in the end. These experiences taught me how to be strong, how to stand up for myself, how to discover my sense of self-worth and purpose, and how to lean on God for a sense of acceptance rather than relying on people. I learned how to stand out rather than seek to fit in during this stage in my life.

Remember: God never said that during the process of becoming who you were meant to become and accomplishing that which you were designed by God to achieve it would be easy. Yes, there will be trials and tribulations; there will be tough times, but regardless of what happens you will make it. Yes, you will. So stand strong and believe in the bright future that God has for you. God has already made way for you.

THE BILLION DOLLAR BABY

CHAPTER 5

The Years My Gift Made Room For Me

I WAS AT THE TOP OF MY GAME ON THE FOOTBALL FIELD. I began playing football, basketball, and running track as a freshman in high school. I also played baseball. I was gifted in sports. I broke every quarterback's passing record in my high school. College scouts began looking at me. During Springtime while in my junior year, I was on the field and was getting ready to punt the football - I was already the punter and the quarterback. I lined up and prepared to kick the football off of the "T" when, all of a sudden, after taking only three steps forward it felt like I had just stepped into a pothole: my tibia and fibula bones in my left leg protruded from my skin. It was the worst injury anyone in my high school had ever seen. You should have seen the faces of my coaches, my players, and the college recruit standing nearby at practice. Some of the teammates had tears in their eyes. I was still in a state of shock, unable to fully feel the pain. My bone was just sticking out of my leg. When I reach down to grab the bone, my leg started turning in a clockwise motion. At that moment, I was overcome with anger towards God. I began to ask God in my mind, "Why me? Why couldn't this happen to someone else? Why me? I'm the guy on my knees all the time! Why not the guy on the sidelines? Why do these type of things always happen to me?" I was angry at God because I felt like He robbed me of a future. I was on my way to playing college football, and this accident happened. I remember riding in the ambulance with the head coach by my side. I asked him and the paramedic, "Will I ever be able to play again?" The look on their faces said it all. The coach and the paramedic just looked at each other silently, then the coach put his hand on my head and said,

"That's not important right now."

"That's not important?!" I yelled. It was important to me. I wanted to hear one of them tell me it's not that bad and that everything was going to be alright. But that's not what was said. The paramedic said it didn't look good and that I'd probably never play again. I cried like a baby. All of my dreams had just slipped away: college scholarships; NFL (National Football League) dreams; etc. They were all gone. At the hospital, Dr. Kelly told me that this injury would take a year to heal. With tears in my eyes, I said, "I don't have a year. This is my senior year coming up." Dr. Kelly went on to inform me that it would take three months of bed rest just for my bones, the skin, the tissue, and the ligaments to heal properly. The doctor then said I would need another nine months of rehab after that. I screamed,

"Nine months?! I don't have nine months!" No amount of arguing back with the doctor was going to change my situation. Interestingly enough, this time I didn't blame my disabilities for holding me back; instead, I began to blame the call of God that was upon my life for my setback. I felt as if God was holding me back. I knew that I was good enough to play in college and the NFL, but I also thought strongly about the fact that God had a different plan for my life than the one I had developed.

What happened to me on that field is what is called a freak accident. The doctor said my leg was pre-cracked. When I went to kick the ball, I applied more pressure on my leg than it could handle; therefore, the bone just exploded. The doctor informed me that the medicine I had been taking all my life had weakened my bones. All of this news had me confused. I didn't know who or what to blame for my predicament; all I knew was I needed to play football again, but things weren't looking so good for me. Desperate, I went to a Friday night healing and deliverance service at Bishop Berry's Church. I had been on bed-rest for roughly two and a half months. I walked into the church on crutches. I wanted God to heal my leg that night. Bishop Barry said he felt like a miracle was in the house for me. I felt as if God gave him a word just for me. I felt strongly in my heart that I was going to receive my healing that night. After Bishop Barry finished praying for me, told me to let the crutches go. At that moment, I threw the crutches down. I then started walking. It felt great. Of course, my mind was on playing football again. Bishop Barry then told me to start running. I started running around and praising

41

God. The church was going crazy. Everyone was praising God for me. When I got home, my leg was hurting so bad I told my mom I needed to go to the doctor. She responded to me saying that I already got my healing. But I told her again that my leg was in intense pain and that I needed to see a doctor. Finally, she took me to the hospital. Once at the hospital, I met with Dr. Kelly who asked me, "What did you do to your leg?" I told him I went to a healing and deliverance service at a church. He retorted "A healing and deliverance service?" with an almost puzzled expression on his face. I said yes. He then asked, "What for?" I told him that I wanted my leg to be healed. He just stared at me for a moment. The expression on his face said it all. At that moment, I began to feel like I had made a dumb decision doing what I did at that deliverance service. And it didn't help to hear what Dr. Kelly had to say after that. He told me that I had re-injured my leg; and because of this, he ordered me back on bed rest for three more months. After hearing that, a knot developed in my stomach. I began to feel sick. Some people would say I didn't have enough faith to believe God for a miracle, but that's not true. That's not the case. The truth is God had performed many miracles in my life before - if you recall, I wasn't supposed to live beyond a few hours at birth. The thing is I didn't seek God for instructions on this matter. I was driven by blind ambition, not faith. I just wanted a quick healing so that I could do what I wanted to do, not what God wanted me to do. I wanted to hurry and get back onto the football field. I cared nothing about God's plan for my life at that time. My blind ambition caused me to move ahead of God's timing.

I was hardheaded and disobedient towards the doctor's orders. I should have set my butt down and rested my leg for those few months as instructed.

The interesting thing about this entire situation is God was secretly setting me up to receive a miracle. After six more months of rest and rehab, I was now able to train myself. Early in the morning during school and after school over the next six months, I worked hard training. I remember cutting a deal with God at this time. All I wanted to do was play football during my senior year of high school, so I promised God that if He allowed me to play football during my senior year, I would preach His Word and do His will. Sure enough, God honored my request. Not only did I recover amazingly and play that year, but I ended up breaking all of my previous records which I set during my sophomore year in passing yards and touchdowns. Now that I was back on the field, I began to think about college football again. My confidence level was rising again. I could see myself winning that football scholarship. During one football game, however, God subtly reminded me of my promise. That game, I was getting ready to punt the ball with my right leg, the leg that had to undergo intense rehab. One of the players on the field decided to target my bad leg on the field, looking to end my career permanently. At that moment, I realized that I had a vow to fulfill. The moment that I made that promise to God flashed right before my eyes. I realized that God had a plan for me to be in the ministry full-time.

I wasn't supposed to live past three days due to my disabilities; and yet, not only did I surpass doctors' expectations, but I went on to do amazing things. I excelled in sports and stood out among my peers. Furthermore, I've been able to preach to my peers in both middle school and high school, and I've prayed for teachers, students, coaches, and athletes. I felt like Moses leading a generation. All of this was practice for something bigger and greater God was getting ready to do in my life. Even with various disabilities, God was using me, showing me favor, and shining His light on me.

When I tell you I was gifted to play football and basketball, understand that that was the case. It came naturally to me. I barely had to practice. This gift stood out to coaches and talent scouts alike. Many times, I would wonder to myself how awesome would I be on the field if I didn't have my condition. I'd imagine myself without the disabilities. The disabilities were like the Apostle Paul's thorn in his flesh. Anytime I wanted to proceed forward in my own strength, my condition was there to remind me that I belonged to God and that my life was not my own. But the role sports played in God's developmental process in my life was they taught me leadership skills; they taught me how to handle people, work on a team, take charge, sacrifice for the team, play my part while others do their part, and focus on the teamwork rather than individuality. These are attributes that it takes to serve in the ministry as I would learn later.

I committed myself to God's purpose for my life. I embraced who God created me to be: a leader. I was a leader on the football and baseball fields, and on the basketball court. I was a leader in my church. I began to be at peace and develop a profound understanding of who I am; and furthermore, I began to love who God made me. I was no longer concerned about who didn't like me. I liked me. I loved me. I stayed surrounded by those who did love and accept me. I felt like a new person. Eventually, other people started to accept me. Coaches and teachers who I knew didn't like me or would just put up with me would begin asking me to pray for them. Some of these people were going through divorces, sicknesses, heartaches, breast cancer, and other issues. It was amazing to see how the very people that negatively talked about me in the beginning were the same ones that were asking me to pray for them and minister to them in the end. Life has a profound sense of irony.

As I stated earlier, the suffering I experienced taught me how to treat other people. I never told my peers about my disabilities; they never asked. As expected, due to many of them not knowing about my disabilities, they judged and criticized me viciously. I endured this only through the grace and power of God. This season of my life developed in me a strong desire to take up for people with problems, disabilities, and shortcomings. In a sense, I felt like it was my job to fight for those who could not fight for themselves. That is still very much a part of me today. God allowed me to grow in His grace, which provided for me the foundation character; this is why, despite my rocky start, I have never allowed bitterness to transform me into a monster. Sure, I got angry, sad, depressed, bitter, and even became suicidal, but there is a light that shines in the darkness and a hope that fills my heart and always allows me to strive to rise above the hurt and pain I feel. I choose to be better, not bitter.

My word to you today is always remember that in-spite of your problems and shortcomings, it's not how you start that matters, it's how you fight through the dark times and finish the race that matters. Here are a few points to take away from this chapter:

- The will of God for your life won't happen if you don't willingly submit to God's plan.
- You don't have to cut a deal with God just follow His will for your life, but you must be willing to accept the possibility that His will for your life may not coincide with the plans you have for yourself.
- Allow God to speak to your heart concerning His plans for your life rather than simply chasing your own wants and desires.
- Faith is not the same as blind ambition and selfish de-sires. Faith is God's will in every situation. God's will comes to pass in our lives when our hearts get into alignment with His wants and desires and we abandon our selfish wants and desires. Yes, God will give us the things we want and desire that are in alignment with His will, but our hearts must first be set on His will and not ours. God's will must become priority, then His blessings will flow.

Part 3
The Plan

CHAPTER 6

The Love Letter That Saved My Life

I WAS NOW A STAR BASKETBALL BASEBALL AND football player in high school. I was being eyed by several colleges, one being the University of Georgia - I was their number three pick. For the first time ever, girls began screaming my name. The same people who use to talk about me were now cheering for me and inviting me to parties; they were asking me to be a part of their cliques, hang out with them in their clubs and homes. Things had turned around for me. I was Mr. Popular now.

At this time, my hormones were raging. I am battling with living the Christian life and "fitting in." This was a real struggle. I found myself trapped between two worlds seemingly: singing and preaching the Word of God on Sundays but Mondays through Saturdays I was living like someone who didn't have a relationship with God - I was busy having sex with girls all throughout the week. One of the things that made my sinful lifestyle so easy to accomplish was the fact that I had been informed my doctor that I could not have children. So, as you'd imagine, not having to worry about impregnating a girl took a lot of stress and worry off of my shoulders and enabled me to keep my sin hidden. I was living two different lifestyles, and nobody knew it. I suspected that some of the girls I was messing with were hoping to get pregnant by a superstar athlete, but I never told them that I couldn't have kids. Even still, I was doing damage to my body by jeopardizing my health by having unprotected sex with multiple partners; and furthermore, I was damaging my soul by harboring in hidden sin.

I have to be honest and tell you that living a secret lifestyle was not all fun and games. The Holy Spirit would convict me often for it, and I'd find myself feeling like a hypocrite. At times, it was difficult to stand before people and preach about living a holy life and serving God after spending the night before living an unholy life and serving my flesh. One lesson my hypocrisy taught me is this: God can use us to bless others while our relationships with Him is out of bounds. Apparently, it's possible for you to preach to others and save their souls while your soul is slated for hell. You should have seen the people in church while I was singing and preaching: they were shouting and dancing and getting blessed. But no one could see how miserable I was. I was secretly dealing with a lot of guilt and shame. While the people were being filled, I was feeling empty. One of the worst moments of my life was the day I was at church ministering the Word of God bold-

ly and I happened to look up and notice one of my class-
mates in the room. She knew about my little secret - my
lifestyle. She was close to some of the girls I was sleeping
with. I was caught red-handed. The look on her face while
I was preaching was enough to make me melt. My heart
dropped into my stomach. I was worried about what she
would think about me, what she would say about me, what
she would say to others around school about me. I couldn't
face her after the service. Afterwards, began conducting
myself carefully and cautiously at school. It was as if I was
walking on eggshells around everyone. That one girl had
me extremely nervous. I knew that she knew God's hand
was on my life; she witnessed it, but she also knew I had a
weakness. But she had a testimony of her own. As it was
well known around campus, she had developed a reputa-
tion for being sexually active and had a child out of wed-
lock at an early age.

It was Monday morning, and I was in the cafete-
ria surrounded by my boys. We were talking about Fri-
day's game and Saturday's girls when the girl from church
walked up to me and smiled. She wasn't the most beautiful
girl in school, but none of us cared about that because we
all knew about her background. She handed me a letter
a letter and then winked at me and told me not to read it
until after school. She told me to wait until I got home to
read it. After she walked away, the guys went crazy on me,
laughing and speculating as to what was in the letter. But
I wanted to follow the girl's instructions, so I waited until
after practice to read the letter. At first, I thought about
stopping by her house before heading home, but I decided

not to. I opened the letter only to be surprised by the fact that it wasn't a love note; instead, it was a reality check. It read:

I know that you thought that this was a love letter about me wanting to sleep with you, but I'm sorry. You're wrong. I would not sleep with a man of God. I'm writing you this letter because I really love you. I saw you at church, and yes, the power of God is on your life, but you are living a hypocritical lifestyle. The same guys at school who you're preaching to are laughing at you behind your back. I heard them. They never knew that I was there. They were dogging you out. They talked about how you preach and sing about God but sleep around with all these girls. They would not tell you to your face. They saw you at that girl's house earlier this morning and leaving late at night. They said you were wearing a suit to school, preaching about God, but you're living like them - sinning.

Calvin, the God in me could not allow you to continue without saying something, especially after seeing God really use you - after seeing the power that was being demonstrated by God through you God and how He was using you to bless others. Yes, this is a love letter for your soul, not to have sex. I pray that you receive this with a great heart.

Signed, your sister in Christ.

I sat in my car with tears strolling down my cheeks. She

was right. I was sad because I knew I was bringing pain to God's heart through my lifestyle. I became mad at my so-called friends and grew frustrated with the devil who I knew was controlling my life through lust. I became upset with myself for living two different lifestyles. Sometimes in life, we struggle with confronting people with the truth, being afraid of what they may think or say about us. In my case, being the superstar athlete, many people weren't going to stand up to me and speak the truth. In reality, a lot of girls wanted to sleep with me and keep me in that sinful lifestyle; my boys weren't going to be honest with me and tell me how they talked about me behind my back, calling me a hypocrite. Most of my peers just wanted my approval and didn't care about the state of my soul. But I'm thankful to God for what I call a real friend, someone who wasn't afraid of what I might say to her when she confronted me with the truth. Of course, she confronted me using wisdom. She didn't come to me and yell in my face, publicly embarrassing me in front of my boys. When you pray and ask God for His guidance in dealing with people, He will give you strategies on how to do so effectively. The letter was appealing, mysterious, and rested on my mind all through school and practice. I couldn't wait to get home to open it. That was a creative way to get the truth to me, one that was non-threatening. But rather than judge me and talk about me behind my back, she was loving enough to correct me. She wasn't afraid of being talked about by my boys. She spoke the truth to a hurting, struggling, backsliding Christian. She saved my life. She showed me the power of real love and reminded me not to allow my flesh to destroy my future and cancel my bright destiny.

Remember: the Word of God says, "For a righteous man falls seven times, and rises again, But the wicked stumble in time of calamity."

CHAPTER 7

Blessed In The Middle Of My Mess

THERE WERE SEVERAL THINGS I DESIRED TO HAVE as a boy growing up; one was a relationship with my father. That missing relationship left a big hole in my life. For fourteen years of my life, I had not spent time with my father. I always felt in my heart that if my father had been there for me, things would have been better in my life. I believed he would have guided me along in my athletic careers and helped me to become a better man. When I turned 18 years old, I went to see my father. I always wondered why he was never there for me. That question, burning in my mind, compelled me to visit him just so that I could get an answer. I didn't care of he got mad at me for asking the question and decided that he never wanted to see me again; I had to know why.

I remember when it was time for me to graduate from high school, I told my grandmother Gladys - my dad's mother - I want my dad to be there. I knew that this would be a risk because my mother did not want him around. But I explained to my mom that this was my day, and I wanted both of them there. I told my mom, "You two have gotten what you wanted it for 18 years now." I felt like now was the time for both my parents to put aside their pride and their animosity and focus on my needs, even if just this one time. I tell parents all of the time when counseling them to be very careful what they do and say because their words and actions can and will affect their kids in the long run. Both of my parents were in the wrong. Neither of them considered how their actions affected me and my brother Keith.

I went to my father's house to talk to him. I had an awesome time. I didn't know what to expect from my dad after fourteen years of his absence, but when I told him I wanted him to be at my graduation ceremony, he was so excited about attending. When graduation day came, I was so excited to see only one face in the audience: my dad's. Other family members were present, but sadly my dad was not. I felt hurt and disappointed. Rumor had it that my dad was going to come to my graduation but backed out of coming after finding out that my mom didn't want him anywhere around us. Before you try to pinpoint blame on someone, just know that to me it didn't matter whose fault it was for my dad not attending my graduation. The only thing that mattered then and even to me now is that he missed one of the most important days of my life.

After the graduation ceremony, I wanted to see my father. I went to see him, not knowing what to expect. I walked up the stairs of his apartment and knocked on the door. "Who is it?" he asked.

"It's Calvin, your son!" I replied from the other side of the door.

"Who?"

"Calvin, your son!"

Dad opened the door and looked at me. When he saw me, he reached out and grabbed me and hugged me. He began to cry while embracing me. Truthfully, I was 6'2 embracing a man who was 6'4, but none of that mattered. I didn't want to let him go. It was as if I was embracing fourteen missing years of my life at that moment. That was the greatest feeling ever. Dad then said to me, "I know that you are having a hard time with me not being there, and I understand it hurts. Please understand that I never forgot about you and your brother. I thought about you guys every day. It was all so hard for me. About not being there for you, please understand it was never meant to be that way. I am sorry. Please forgive me. Yes, I have messed up, and I've made many mistakes and bad choices by you and your mother. But you are my son. You look like me. You walk like me. You talk like me. I miss you and your brother, Keith. I love both of you guys, and one day you will know the whole truth about me. Believe it or not, I know all of your stats. I know the colleges that want you. I've always kept up with you. I tell people all the time that Calvin Ward is my son. They say, 'Jr., that's not your boy.' I told them, 'His name is really Calvin Jones. That's my son.'" He then said, "Let's take a ride to the corner store." We jumped into the car, drove to Washington Road, and hopped out the car. Left and right, people were calling my dad's name: "Hey, Junior!" Dad spoke to everyone. I could hear someone asking,

"Junior, who is that handsome man with you? He looks just like you."

"This is my son, the one I've been telling you all about!" dad answered. He indeed had been talking about me to everyone. He was so proud to announce to everyone that I was his son. Those few hours I spent with my father were some of my fondest memories.

The time had come for me to leave. I took dad back home. While driving, he leaned over and made this statement to me, which I never forgot: "One day, you will know the truth." At the time, I didn't fully understand what that meant. To his credit, my dad had never spoken one negative word against my mom, at least not to me. Once at his house, I told my father that I wanted to get married, but I wanted him to meet my girlfriend first. He was excited about meeting her. At the time, I was dating a young lady named Keiyawna. For me, this was the one. She loved God and was just my type. I later took her over to see my dad. The excitement on my dad's face was incredible. It was amazing to me to see how I and my dad's relationship was beginning to bloom. Everything was beginning to look great for the two of us. And then, all of a sudden, it happened: I received one of those dreaded phone calls while I was at work stating that my father has slipped into a diabetic coma. My heart dropped at that moment. Just when things were starting to look great for my dad and me, suddenly this happened. The doctor told me that my dad was on a breathing machine. They said even if he lived, he would have been brain dead. I was completely crushed by this.

Neither I nor any of my siblings were allowed to make the final decision regarding my dad: whether or not to pull the plug on him or keep him alive to remain in his comatose state. That decision was left up to his next to kin, which was his oldest child which he had outside of he and my mother's relationship. This was a hard decision that had to be made. All of us, his children, talked about it. After much prayer, my heart was content with this one decision: it was best to pull the plug. We all agreed. After we made the decision, I left the hospital - it was around 12 am when I left. Around 2 am, that's when I received a phone call stating that dad had passed. I did not call anyone the rest of that morning. I waited until daybreak to tell the rest of my family the news. Losing touch with my father for fourteen years of my life was hard, but not like this. This time, my father was gone forever. I would never be able to create memorable moments with him. My life brother Keith was angry over the fact that he and dad never really got the chance to reconcile and make peace as I had done.

After the funeral, I received another phone call saying that everything my father owned, he left it to me. It amazed me because I was the child he didn't want to claim ownership over at birth, I'm the one he rejected the most. Truthfully, my father didn't own much. But what I gathered from the situation was he was trying to convey this message to me: Calvin, I didn't do much for you in the beginning, but I want to make up for all that I didn't do for you. Things that meant the world to him, he left with me. The first possession of my dad's that I explored was his black bag, which contained a lot of papers he hadn't shown to me. I opened the bag and I started reading through the papers. What I read broke my heart. I discovered that dad couldn't read very well; he made a lot of bad choices by my mother, some of which landed him in jail. After not being able to pay child support, he also became a product of the system. He would work as a laborer, which only paid him $7 - $10 a week. I also found ISO applications that had been filled out for fourteen years straight, and artsy drawings with my name on them and my brother Keith name on it. At that moment, that's when it hit me. I finally figured out what he meant when he told me that one day I'd discover the truth. It wasn't that he didn't want to pay child support; he simply didn't have it. Some would say it was his fault for being in the situation he was in, which is true. Yes, there were things he could have done differently, but his unfortunate circumstance made me think about the eighteen years we missed and how bad decisions were able to rob us of that time. I learned several lessons from his experience:

Lesson #1: Never hold in issues that can be resolved through communication.
Lesson #2: Things are never as bad as they seem.
Lesson #3: Time is short. Don't allow hate and un-forgiveness to keep you from experiencing the peace and happiness you deserve.

I graduated from high school despite being born with one of the rarest abnormalities on the planet. I struggled in school and life due to my medical issues. I had three disabilities in my kidneys, my bladder, and my bowels. I did my best to live a normal life, knowing all the while that I was anything but normal. I was the one who wasn't supposed to make it, the one who was counted out upon birth. Now, I am graduating from high school.

I didn't go on to play football at the University of Georgia because I broke my leg, and my coaches told the recruiters. But by then, I had fallen in love with the ministry and preferred to preach the Gospel more than playing football. I went to a small college in South Georgia with my girlfriend. Secretly, I was a little upset, angry, and frustrated over not being recruited by the University of Georgia because I knew I could play football at the highest level, but I also knew in my heart that I had a call of ministry on my life and I made a promise to God. My girlfriend at the time, Keiyawna, was about forty-five minutes away. I went to visit her, and one thing led to another: we conceived a child. I messed up big time. When conception occurred, I knew it; something was different; I felt it in my heart, in my gut. Later on, it was confirmed when a few months later, Keiyawna called me and told me she was pregnant. "Pregnant?!" I asked. She already had one daughter; and now, she's getting ready to have my baby. It didn't make sense to me at first because the doctor told me I couldn't have any kids. But then, I started thinking about the fact that the doctor also said that I wouldn't live beyond childbirth; and yet, I lived. How many times was the doctor wrong? The doctor told me that I wouldn't be able to play ball and do many of the things I went on to do. So, now, I couldn't rule out the idea that I could be the father of this baby. I then began to worry about what God thought about me. I began to worry about what others would say about me.

I remember it like it was yesterday: my mother called me at four o'clock in the morning. She sounded like she had been up all night. She asked me, "What's going on?" I said,

"Well, it's four o'clock in the morning - what do you think?"

"I know something is wrong, so you may as well tell me now," she responded.

"I feel well, but Keiyawna is pregnant." It's amazing how our parents can sense things without us telling them.

One of the first thoughts that crossed my mind after the news of my girlfriend's pregnancy was how was I going to break the news to my church family. I was very active in my church. I was a minister. I feared that they would crucify me for having sex outside of marriage and having a baby out of wedlock. After telling the pastor, he made me stand before the entire congregation and confess my sins. After that, I was sat down from all of my activities and duties in the church. Many of the people began to criticize and blame my girlfriend for the entire situation because she had already had a child before even reaching the age of eighteen. But it wasn't her fault; it was mine. While people were judging and criticizing her, they were oblivious to the fact that it was I who was living a double-life. I talked her into having sex with me. I initiated the whole thing.

I was back in a low place, a low point in my life. It was painful: having people look down on me, hearing people criticize me for my sins and mistakes and call me a big sinner. What pained me, even more, was the fact that many of the people talking about my sin were in the same boat as me...or worst. I knew about the personal demons many of the church members wrestled with: two of the ministers there were sleeping around with church members and getting drunk occasionally; many of the deacons had a smoking habit; many of the musicians were sleeping around with the members, especially the choir members; members sleeping around with each other; the church mothers were gossiping on and hating on each other behind their backs. It seemed hypocritical that everyone was targeting me rather than addressing their sins also. Why was I the only one that had to stand before the congregation? Oh, I know why: I just happened to be the one that got caught.

These types of things going on in churches all across the nation. Truthfully, none of us are living a perfect life. We are all experiencing some weakness, engaging in some sin, and possess some dysfunction. No one is perfect and is sinless. That is why the Bible prescribes compassion and mercy for us. The Bible tells us that if we plant forgiveness and mercy in the lives of others when the day comes when we fall we will receive mercy in return. That's what the Bible means when it tells us to "judge not lest we be judged." It's not saying we must condone sin and give it a free pass; it's saying we must not condemn the sinner, but recognize that we're all in need of mercy and must help one another to go higher.

After this, my girlfriend became my wife. It was now me, my wife, Keiyawna, and our two beautiful girls, Kahleighya and Kemia. We were now one big happy family. And I must admit that after having gotten married, my sexual appetite was now in check. That is the benefit of having a spouse.

I remember sitting down one Sunday evening and asking God how could I receive a blessing from the mess that I created. If all things work together for our good when we love God, then I needed God to show me how my disabilities were going to work together for my good, and I also needed Him to help me see my way in the midst of all that I was in. And God answered me. He showed me that despite my disabilities, He sent me someone to love me, He spared my life, He protected me throughout all of those years I was having unprotected sex with multiple girls, He allowed me to defy expectations and accomplish things that medical doctors said I'd never accomplish, and lastly, He gave me a child when the doctors said I'd never be able to have children. Not only that, but God proved His power in my life by allowing me to go on to have two more children after our first daughter together.

My word to you today is this: We all make mistakes and mess up in life, but keep your trust in God and know that He has a plan for you and that it doesn't matter what others think or say about you - what matters is what you think and say about yourself and that you don't identify yourself as a failure or a screw-up. Remember that all things are working together for your good.

Part 4

the Pursuit

Chapter 8

It Cost Me My Life

I REMEMBER WHEN I WAS 12 YEARS OLD, I WAS playing on what I considered to be the best little league baseball team ever. We were not the best because we had the greatest players; it was because we played hard and always finished strong. We played the Reds who had the best overall players in the league. This was the championship game; it was my night to pitch against my friends and other great ballplayers. These were some of the greatest players I've ever faced. We came to the field with our green shirts, white pants, and green hats. We were the Wallace Park A's. It was my time to shine. I had to pitch a no-hitter in order for us to win. I was pitching no-hitters thus far. I had hit a solo home run. We were winning the game 1-0. You could feel the energy at the top of the fifth inning. The game only went to seven innings. I was pitching the game of my life. I went back to throw the next pitch, and I felt something in my stomach. Oh no! I know this feeling all too well, I thought to myself. Yep. As you can imagine, I had a bowel movement on myself and messed all over my white pants while everyone was watching. All eyes were on me. You should have heard the screams from teammates and other kids yelling to "Run!!!" My peers, my teammates, and even the adults were saying horrible things about me at that moment. Now, you probably are thinking that I just left the field and went somewhere and cried my eyes out after that, but I didn't. Strangely enough, I was actually committing to finishing the game strong and leading my team to victory. Still, I had to leave the game. I wasn't allowed to return to the field because I didn't have a change of clothes. The coach replaced me with another teammate. While my replacement was on the field, the opposing team, The Reds, began to take the lead over us. I was still determined, however, to get on the field and help our team score a victory, so I cleaned my clothes real good and then assured my teammates not to worry because I was back and ready to finish the game strong. We gave it our best shot, but still lost the game 3-1. The Reds won the championship.

We could have won that game. In my mind, we should have won the game. But win, lose, or draw, I still felt like a winner through this experience. I believe this was a God-ordained situation in my life designed to put my life, my courage, my resolve on display before the world. In this situation, others were able to see the power of determination, and how one can "stay in the game" even when things don't look good for them, even when they're plagued by many shortcomings. In that moment, it wasn't about who won, it was about who didn't give up. Likewise, you shouldn't allow your shortcomings and issues to make you quite and give up on this game called life. Just learn how to clean up your mess and get back on the field. Keep playing ball. Was I embarrassed by what happened to me on the field? Of course. But despite how embarrassed I was, I was more concerned about my teammates that I was my self-image. I put the team first, before myself. If we were going to lose that championship game, I was determined that it would not be said we lost because I was incapable of leading due to my own personal issues. I didn't want the lost to be blamed on me. I acknowledged the things that were beyond my control, but was determined to do what I was capable of doing to finish the game strong. Amazingly, although we lost the game, I won over the hearts and minds of the onlookers. My team and I won the respect of those around us. People were actually saying we won over the city, and that we scored a spiritual victory that day.

If you're going to remain in the game, it's important that you discover how handle being at your lowest point. While on that baseball field, I found myself at a low point. Embarrassed. Humiliated. Being mocked and scorned. Being treated like a disease. And yet, in the midst of all of this, my action was to encourage others when I myself needed encouragement. Like I discovered on that field, it wasn't about winning the game; but rather, it was about winning over the hearts and souls of others. As a Christian, I realize that the most important goal in life is to win souls for Christ. By putting my eyes on the right goal, I was able to walk away without a trophy and still maintain a strong sense of pride and a positive self-esteem. I walked away with my head held high in the midst of it all. I rose above my self-image and put the needs of others first. I didn't let my team down. I didn't let my coaches down. I didn't let the parents and onlookers down. Some of them were compassionate over my situation. They were informing the other parents in the audience who were gasping in horror over the sight of my pants being stained that I had a condition, a disability, and couldn't control myself. At that moment, they began to understand all the more what was happening and respect the fact that I didn't let my personal shame prevent me from finishing the game. They were inspired by my actions.

I learned through that experience to not allow a disability control me; but rather, I needed to take control over the disability. I learned not to allow a disability to defeat me in my mind. Everyone in life has some sort of disability. Everyone has some area in their lives where they suffer a weakness. Some people may have a mental weakness, others a physical disability. But know that we all have one. All of us are born with a spiritual disability that can only be healed by the grace and power of God. All of us will find ourselves facing moments of great weakness—facing low points. We'll all find ourselves dealing with mess that's beyond our control. But I want to encourage you to not allow your circumstances to mentally control you. Leave the things that are beyond your control in God's hands and do the things you can to improve the situation.

There are four principles that have become a guiding light in my life. These principles are:

1. It is important that you dream. Everyone should

have a dream. Our dreams begin in our minds; they start with our imaginations. Our thoughts rule in our minds; they run our heads. Many people have not succeeded because they haven't first envisioned and imagined themselves winning. But once you get a vision of yourself winning, you'll become unstoppable. Anyone can dream. It doesn't matter if you're young, old, healthy, disabled, all of us can dream. You don't have to be wealthy to dream. You can dream where you are, in the situation you're in. Dream big dreams.

2. Acknowledge and act on your desires. There is a difference between a desire and a dream. A dream is confined to what's in your head, but a desire allows you to act upon that dream. Many people simply live in their heads but don't pursue their dreams. You must chase after your dreams if you're going to experience them. I've never allowed myself to suffer from a dream deferred. In other words, even if I didn't get what I wanted, I never made excuses for not pursuing after it. Even if I failed, I always made sure that I could say at least I tried. When you desire something, you'll begin to put together a plan of action to experience that dream; you won't allow anything to stop you, not obstacles, disabilities, emotions; nothing; furthermore, you won't allow yourself to stop you. Let your dreams become desires.

3. You must be driven in life. You must have a certain "Why" or "What" that keeps you going. Why do you want to be great? What is pushing you to greatness? What is your motivation, your reason for doing what you do? These are the questions I had to ask myself. No one else can answer these questions for you. You must answer them for yourself. Only you know what's in your heart. I wanted to become great. I did not want to live off excuses. I did not want to live off of pity. That was my "why" in life. Later on in life, my "what" became my family—my wife. The thought of her pushed me to do greater things in life, to keep going despite my shortcomings. I became determined to give her the best in life. I wanted her to see not my disabilities, but my abilities. God blessed me with a beautiful wife with a huge heart, one who gave birth to my "miracle children" (if you recall, I was told by doctors that I would never have children; and yet, I stand today with children of my own, from my own loins). I wanted my children to have the best, be the best, and to know that there is nothing in life that they cannot have as long as the plan to finish strong. You have to have a goal before your eyes that you can work towards; this will produce a drive in you to push through the pain. When you have a drive, nothing can stop you.

4. Know that you have a great destiny. Destiny is the place where your dreams and realized and mani-

fested. You can only reach this place if you continue to push forward. Yes, God is the one who decides your future, but you have to be willing to push towards the will of God for your life. Most of us don't know what the future holds, but we are aware of the dreams that are in our hearts. Your destiny is not a house, a car, or money in the bank; it is the plan of God for your life. Your destiny deals with who you are, who God made you. Sure, we want and need material things in this life, but the Bible tells us to chase after God and His righteousness and then we'll see these things be added unto our lives. I encourage everyone to spend time discovering the will of God for their lives, to discover the purpose for why they were created. Do you know your purpose? When you know your God-given purpose in life, you won't allow your shortcomings and disabilities to prevent you from pursuing and reaching your destiny. You weren't designed to be trapped by a disability; you were designed to chase after your destiny. Don't compare yourself to others. Don't judge yourself by your shortcomings. Keep your eyes on your destiny. Realize the stage of life that you're in and learn to manage there. Some of us may be in the dreaming stage; some of us in the desire stage; some of us in the drive stage, but never quit.

THE BILLION DOLLAR BABY

CHAPTER 9

Hiding The Hurt Hurts The Most

T HERE ARE SOME SITUATIONS FROM MY PAST THAT stand out in my mind, one being the day I had to go to the hospital due to a kidney infection. During this time, I was playing baseball. The time for me to go to the hospital was around the same time as picture day for my baseball team. Three days before I was admitted to the hospital, the doctors told me that I could not play in Saturday's game. "You don't understand," I told the doctor, "my team needs me, and I have never missed a game. I'm the leader of the team, and I can not let my team down."

"Son, you're too weak, and your kidney is damaged," the doctor replied. In my heart, I knew he was right, but in my mind, I was not trying to hear it. I cried and cried and cried. I then asked the doctor if I could at least take a picture with my team? He agreed and allowed me to spend at least three hours with my team to take pictures. I was so happy. I was smiling from ear to ear. Of course, I knew my teammates would be inquisitive as to why I wasn't playing with them on the field. I wasn't prepared for the pain of not being able to play with them in the game either. I was smiling on the outside but internally crushed. I still had the IV in my arm when I took the pictures.

I learned during this time to never take anything for granted because at any time we can lose everything that we have, including the use of our limbs. Just three days before the game, I was feeling fine; and now, I'm in a hospital room due to a kidney infection. I had to force myself to smile even though I was in pain both physically and emotionally. It's amazing how people will see you smile and automatically assume that everything is okay, never realizing that smiles often hide our pain. For many years, no one asked me how I "really" felt during the different situations I experienced; no one asked me about my mental state when going through. People just wanted so desperately for me to smile so that they wouldn't have to deal with the burden of my troubled heart. As long as I was smiling, everyone was fine and comfortable. Hiding your feelings won't make them go away. Time doesn't heal pain. It's interesting that the same pain that I felt when I was a child is the same pain I feel today. As much as I try to smile and make people feel comfortable around me, I still long for those moments when I can get alone and let out my feelings. I talk to God about my feelings. I talk to myself about how I'm feeling. I just have to get it out. I let the people see the smile, my strength, the soldier who is a fighter; that's the "me" I let everyone see. But when

I'm alone, I can let the guard down and take off the mask and be honest. I feel so free during these times of openness and emotional honesty. I've learned to be honest with myself and acknowledge my emotions. Having an emotion doesn't make you a bad person. Whether or not you are angry with yourself, others, or God; whether or not you're feeling ashamed, embarrassed, humiliated, afraid, suspicious, etc., it doesn't matter. What matters is that you find that time to connect with your emotions and express them to God. I've always said that I don't want people to feel sorry for me, but that doesn't mean I didn't want anyone to care about me and how I feel. I remember preaching to the inmates in a local jail once. The inmates just stared at me, showing no emotions the whole time I was up ministering. I felt like I wasn't connecting with them like I was boring them to death. But after the service, I was amazed to see how many of the inmates were coming up to me and telling me how much they enjoyed the message. At that moment, I realized that you can't judge a book by its cover. Just because a person isn't showing any emotions, that doesn't mean they're not experiencing any emotions.

I was only 19 years old when I got my girlfriend Keiyawna pregnant. I was receiving a disability check through Medicaid. I made up my mind that I wanted to marry Keiyawna, the love of my life. A family member told me that if I got married, I would lose my disability check and insurance. This made me think that there was no other option for me besides finding a job and working the best that I could to provide for my family. I was troubled by this because I knew that my disability would be an issue. I did what was necessary, however, and I got a job. Now, I was no longer receiving a disability check. Now that I wasn't receiving assistance, my family and I struggled; furthermore, my struggle was intensified by the fact that I had to work to hide the terrible smells that were in my clothes day after day. I was always in the restroom trying to hide from everyone. I was later shocked when one of my family members informed me that it wasn't true that I'd lose my disability if I started working. At that point, I thought about how my family and I needlessly suffered as a result of me giving up one stream of income. My family and I would have benefited from my disability check. It may not have been much for me to receive my adult's portion and my children to receive their child's portion, but it would have brought peace into my life at that time, and my family would have been taken care of. I wouldn't have had to deal with the stress, disappointment, and depression of not being able to provide and take care of my family.

I never dealt with the medical terminology of my disabilities. I never knew that medically, what I was suffering from was called a kidney disease. I was never told this by my family or the doctors; so when I filled out job applications, I always said I did not have a kidney disease. It wasn't until September 29th, 2015 that I actually went and read the medical terms for the disabilities I was suffering with. When I looked up the medical term for each disability and what they were worth - how much money I was supposed to receive for each disability - you should have seen the look on my face.

After graduating from high school and getting married to Keiyawna, I began working at a car dealership. The first month of being there, I was the second-highest car salesman in the whole dealership. The next month, I was the #1 salesman. The problem was I was never at home, and it created a conflict with my family and I. Also, my job was pulling me away from my church. It was hard living the car salesman's lifestyle on Monday through Saturday and most times on Sunday evening and ministering on Sunday morning trying to live for God. Eventually, I left the car dealership and started working at a mattress company. It was hard because this was a production company - you had to always be in place, on the assembly line, and they counted on you every second of every minute. The times that I had to go to the restroom, it held up everyone else. This change in career was hard for me alongside with losing about $30,000 a year. I was struggling. My family was struggling. I felt like a loser, a failing father, a failing husband. I never had a father figure to pattern myself after and show me how to be a husband and a father. I was trying to grab examples of fathering and being a husband from all of the positive men that were in my life. I looked at my uncles Allen, Pastor Harden, and a man named John Kelly. Thank God for these examples. I was so lost, I didn't know what to do or where to go from there. I didn't know how to get my family on the right track. One day, I went to my nephews Kyle and Taylor's baseball games. It was like God sent us a miracle in the form of a man named Willie Burge. I believe Willie saw the hurt in my eyes. The Word of God says you can see a man's soul through his eyes. Well, that day, my soul was hurting. Willie was one of the top managers at a major power company in the state of Georgia. I told Willie a little bit of my story. I shared with him how after getting married my family began to struggle. I informed him that my wife was pregnant and that we already had a one-year-old. I told him that I wanted to work and that I tried my best and I just needed a chance. No one else besides my wife knew that my disability check was soon to run out. The clock was ticking. I was crying, even weeping. In my time alone, I was trying to figure out life, not knowing that Keiyawna was observing me as a husband, as a father, and as a provider. Deep down within, I purposed that I wouldn't be like Junior, my dad. I wanted my kids to have a better life then my brother Keith and I. I wanted them to be able to get the things that they wanted and not be concerned about whether or not we could afford it. I didn't want my wife to have to struggle from day to day. Willie told me exactly what to do. I went to fill out the job application. When I got to the question "Do I have a kidney disease?" I put "No". I knew that I had problems with my kidneys, but I was never informed of the severity of my problem; so I was under the assumption that I didn't havea kidney disease. Still, I wanted to hide the fact that I did have issues with my kidneys, figuring that as long as no one else knew about my condition it was fine to hide it. I wanted and needed to work. This job was a whole new world to me. The company started me out making more money than I made at the dealership and the mattress company. I had Insurance, a 401k; I had the best benefits; it was like God blessed me beyond measure. This was what I always dreamed of. My family and I were finally able to purchase our first house and our first brand new car. We were now living in the best school district. The life that I prayed for, we finally had. Everything was great. We were a normal family. I was able to go to church and continue to minister. My wife was able to do whatever she wanted to do; she could pursue the career of her choice. I was normal - at least, that's what I told myself. The truth is, I knew in my heart that I wasn't normal. But I decided that I was going to ride out this job for as long as my body would hold up.

The job was beginning to get harder. The bosses would ask me to climb trees. I still had issues with my bowel movements. At times, I would mess on myself and the crew members would just laugh at me. The crew members would talk about me. I would just hang my head in shame. But as long as my family had food to eat and a roof over their heads, that's what mattered the most.

Working on a five-man crew was one of the hardest things I had ever done. I felt the need to be by myself, to be alone. On those days when it was extremely hot outside, those were the worst times - the smell in that truck would be unbearable. On the cold days, we would freeze because no one could take the smell. Sometimes, the other crew members would pile into one truck, choosing to be uncomfortably jammed together just so that they didn't have to ride in the truck with me. I would find myself riding all alone. They would ask me to dig dirt out of a hole so that we could load the pipes for the power lines in the ground; I would sit down in the dirt just to cover up the stains in my clothes. I was trying to hide what everyone knew but was afraid to acknowledge. No one would talk about it to my face; everyone would, however, talk about what was going on with me behind my back. All I could do was focus on my family - on making sure that I continued to provide food, shelter, and all of their needs. As long as they were happy and smiling, everything was okay. Still, I was hurt on the inside because of the whole situation. You probably wouldn't have been able to tell I was hurting deeply because I was good at covering up my pain with a smile, but the pain ran deep in my heart.

I never talked to my wife about the things that I was going through on the job. To a degree, I felt as if it wasn't all that big of an issue. I didn't feel the need to add more stress to her. Our young marriage had been under enough strain as it was. I didn't even tell her the whole truth about all of my disabilities. I was too ashamed to reveal to her everything I was dealing with. I was afraid that she would look at me differently if I told her everything. I wanted her to continue to see me as the tall, funny, clean, handsome guy that she saw and fell head over heels for when we first met in Powder Springs, Georgia at a church dinner. I remember the day she told her oldest daughter to approach me and call me "Dad" just to see how I'd respond. I remember saying to Keiyawna's mother while Keiyawna was standing next to her, "Is that your sister?" You should have seen the smile on her mother's face. She took an instant liking to me. I needed my wife to remember that Calvin, not the disabled and hurting Calvin. So, yes, I became skilled at hiding my true feelings and even hiding the truth about myself. I grew skilled at creating a facade. I had been raised all my life not to act and think like I was disabled. My family didn't want to acknowledge that I was disabled. So, when I confronted with people treating me a certain way due to my disabilities, I did not know how to respond. Now, here I was faced with the challenge of revealing a truth my family tried to hide from me, and I tried to hide from everyone else. I didn't know if this truth would drive Keiyawna away from me or bring her closer to me. All I knew was I didn't want to lose her. I knew I had gained more than just a wife and child; I gained an angel, a gift from God. I had someone to bring the best out of me. She gave me something I never had before, something to live for, and something to fight for.

My wife had become my best friend. Up until then, my best friend was my brother Keith. I could tell him anything. Keith understood me; and if he didn't understand something about me, he would pretend to understand me. Now, God has blessed me with a beautiful wife who loved me even after I began to unveil my issues. Keiyawna was a dream come true, the mother of my miracle child, the woman who gave me a family, but she was meant to be more than just a wife; she was meant to be my confidant. I sensed that it was time to open up to her and let her see the real Calvin. I had started to open up to my wife. I had started to talk to Keiyawna about my issues, and she accepted me still. She stuck by my side for years. She never judged me. She never put me down. She never talked about me. She always took care of me. She cooks, she cleans, she washes my clothes, and she sees to my needs. She has never made fun of my disabilities. Because of this, my desire was and is to give Keiyawna the world. She is my friend who has always supported my dreams and passions, a friend who has been there during the good times and the bad times, the one who witnessed my highest moments and my lowest moments. She saved my life. She did.

Keiyawna told me one day that I can preach all over the world, saving, healing, and delivering lives, but if I don't take care of myself, I'll be no good to anyone else. That moment, I decided to take my medicine, catheterize myself, and do my best to manage my bowels. Her words pierced my heart. From that day forward, I gained new strength and courage to go to the power company and work. It was tough; it was hard. I had many bad days, but nothing in the world could stop me from being there for my family. God taught me how to release the hurt. I realized that by holding on to the hurt in my heart, I was hurting myself and everyone connected with me. Learn how to face what hurts you the most. Don't worry about what people say, think, and do; just focus on getting your heart healed. The word of God says we triumph over the devil by the blood of the lamb and the word of our testimony (Revelation 12:11). When I started to realize this, I started to heal and release the hurt. When I started to let it out and talk about it, I began to overcome the hurt and disappointment from the past and the present in my life.

Why is hiding your hurt destructive? One reason is that by doing so, you mislead those around you. I learned to smile and act like everything was okay, and this misleads people. When I tell people that I've always been disabled from a child up, most people don't believe me; many people have a hard to believing me; some people will say they never knew it or would have believed it by the way I look. My encouragement to you is this: Always smile, even when you're hurting, but don't carry the hurt in your heart for a long time like I did. I carried my hurt around for over 30 years. Don't even hold on to it for 30 minutes. Get it out. Talk to someone. Share what's going on in your heart with those who're close to you. There is nothing like a heart that's hurting. Some people have grown skilled at encouraging others and helping them to heal their hearts while they, themselves, still carry broken hearts. Many people try to hurt others because their hearts are hurting. As the old saying goes: Hurt people will hurt people. I'd like to add that healed people will try to help people heal. What type of person do you want to be: the one who hurts others or the one who helps others to heal? When you make it a habit of hiding your hurt and pain, you increase the chances of becoming the individual who hurts others rather than helps them heal.

Confess your hurt. Release your pain. Move past the hurt and pain.

I know this may sound crazy, but I'm glad I was hurt at a young age by my family and friends. Why? It taught me not to blindly trust and count on everyone. I learned that some people you may be counting on aren't worthy of your trust. Be careful what you ask for. The Lord taught me a valuable lesson one day. I am a man of faith already. Everything I have ever needed God has supplied. He has kept me alive. God kept me all throughout elementary, middle, and high school. He protected me from people who were picking on me. God kept me from church hurt and let downs. I have never been homeless. I have always had my needs met. My wife loves me. My kids love me. My mother and my brother have always been there for me. On September 29th, God called me off of my job - I was totally and permanently disabled. I provided the best that I could for my family. Can you imagine that for over seventeen years I had been able to feel a real sense of joy and that my heart was hurting even while I smiled at everyone around me? It was funny: I went to the doctor one day, and on the questionnaire, for the first time I was asked this question: "How would you feel if you had to live with your condition the rest of your life?" I smiled. I didn't answer the question because I knew that the doctor would not understand my answer. I asked God, "Are you sure, Lord?" It was time for me to leave the job. I was making about $30 an hour, and it all came to an end on September 29th. I had a plan. I had it all worked out. But what I didn't know was God had another plan for me.

For the first six months, we did everything we could with the finances we had. We paid off most of our major bills and anyone that we owed: companies, credit cards, etc. We made sure that there was a zero balance on all of our accounts. The Lord allowed us to pay off our cars. We were careful not to blow our money. I knew that there would come a time when we'd need help down the road. There were about ten people I decided to open up my heart to and tell that I needed some help. I had never asked anyone of them for help; I hardly asked anyone at all for anything up until this point. But you would have thought that I was asking for a free ride. This act bothered me because I knew in my heart the things that I did for these individuals in the past. Anytime they'd ask me to do something or give them something, I was there for them, but when I needed them, they weren't there. What do you do when the people you count on when at your lowest point are unreliable? I had to beg for bill money, gas money, and money for things my kids needed. When some people would call to check up on me, I wanted to hang up the phone although my heart wouldn't allow me to. No one owed me anything; I simply thought that I could count on my close family and friends. During this time, the Lord spoke to me and said, "This season of your life is called 'walking by faith.'" This season was me totally depending on God. I had no job and no income; and yet, I still had to preach the Word of God to the people of God; I still had to encourage others by reminding them that God was going to supply for them and bless them and that everything was going to be okay while I was struggling and needed encouragement and help. I stopped asking people for help. I began to depend on God. The only one that I could count on was the one that I started counting on. God became my source, my provider, my way maker. I just remember saying God would make a way when situations arose. I use to get angry whenever people didn't give to those in need, but as time progressed I started to see things differently - I realized that we should be relying on God because He is in control. This revelation was preparing me for my next lesson. God was preparing me for my next level of faith, one that would affect my family and my ministry. This experience taught me how to love people who didn't like me and move forward without the people who didn't want to help me. I'd ask God, "Lord, how much longer will this go on?" I would always hear God say, "Son, until you pass the faith test."

My faith and testimony grew stronger due to this season of my life. Many times before, I would hear the saying "Walk by faith and not by sight" and just assume that I understood what that meant, but this time this saying took on a whole new meaning. I really had to walk by faith. At one of my lowest points, I can truly say that my wife stuck by my side through it all. I know that many times she just wanted to scream at God and me, "What are you doing?!!! What is all of this about?!!!" But she stayed faithful. I believe that we grew closer as a family because of this experience. My kids were understanding and accepting of the situation. Now, that's not to say they enjoyed this season of our lives, but they understood that God was teaching us a lesson. My wife took a job working at UPS to help make ends meet. Her working there made me sick to my stomach. But she did what she could to help us stay afloat. One of the greatest lessons I discovered during this season of my life is to count on God and He will allow your every moment to count. If you and your family pull close during the trying times, everything will work out, especially for those who trust God. You can count on God; He'll never let you down.

CHAPTER 10

I Would Still Pay The Price

I WAS TWENTY YEARS OLD, DISABLED, AND MARRIED with three beautiful girls: Kahleighya, Kemia, Kaela. Although I was disabled, my mother and my grandmother ("Ma") never told me that I was disabled; they always treated me like I was normal like the other kids. I thought I had to do what other married people did, which was to get a job and to provide for my family. The difference-maker, however, was my bowels, my kidneys, and my bladder - they didn't work properly. Due to me having bowel movements on myself and having to catheterize myself, I was always trying to find the right job, one that fit my needs. I received the Social Security Identification check until I was twenty years old; after that, that check was cut off. I never thought to stay on because I really didn't think that was an option. I simply attempted to do my best with my disability to provide for my family. Many times, I didn't realize that people were talking about me. Wherever I would go to work, it was déjà vu all over again.

Keiyawna and I live the Christian lifestyle. We don't drink, don't smoke, don't hang out at the clubs; I'm pastoring a church and working our kids who are doing great. From the world's point of view, we're living a pretty boring life, but from God's point of view, we're on our way to heaven. I'd be lying to you if I told you that we didn't contemplate doing a few worldly things, but we decided to remain holy "as unto the Lord," knowing that one day, everything will pay off for us on earth and in heaven. After working to the point where I could no longer work due to my disabilities, my faith remained strong. I knew then just like I know now that if God made a way for me before, He can and will make a way for me again.

I was talking to my spiritual father, Dr. Barns. I told him I was the only child and the only person that lives in the United States of America with my condition. I told him that someone needs to hear my story so that they'd believe in miracles. I told him that I wanted others to be blessed with my life's story. I am called to help the world know that no matter how bad things get in life God can heal you, take care of you, and provide for you. God can save you and protect you even when things seem like they're not going to work out. God will send a Dr. Rickets as a blessing to reconstruct your situation so that you can bless the state, nation, and the world.

I am a walking, talking, living testimony. Yes, there is no doubt about it. Sure, being a testimony caused me much heartache and pain, but it was all worth it after seeing how my life and story has touched, changed, and blessed so many others with the help of the Lord.

Being 36 yrs. old, I was living with reduced abilities from birth, one being an Imperforate Anus with a post-pull through Rectal Agenda and a Colostomy Retroprostate Fistula Repair. The second clinical indication is Congenital Genitourinary Abnormalities and Neurogenic Bladder; the third is Hydronephrosis with Cortical Thinning. These conditions are what I deal with every day: bad kidneys, a very bad bladder, and bowels that don't work. This is the price that I have to pay to be a testimony. Many people will probably never know about my situation; many people can't tell that there is something wrong with me until they smell something horrible. After receiving a disability check all the way until the age of twenty, I still chose to get married. Then it was told to me that I would lose my disability benefits if I got married. I did not want that check to stop me from pursuing what God had for me. I never wanted money to stop me from getting married, so I went to work. I'm married with three girls. I no longer receive that check from social security for my disabilities; and yes, my condition continues to persist, and is getting worse. I didn't know that I was making a huge mistake by choosing to work rather than continue to receive a check to take care of my family. I thought I was doing the best thing for my family at the time.

What I did was give up my rights as one who was and is disabled as a result of being advised wrongfully. After suffering from job to job, keeping my mouth closed about my disabilities, I landed a job with one of the local power companies; it was a great paying job, but it was trouble on my mind and body. I felt so ashamed of not being able to control my bowels and smelling up the trucks whenever riding with the crew members. I knew that they knew the horrible smells were coming from me; they'd noticed that my pants were often stained with brown stains and were wet; this went on for many years. What I didn't know at the time was the company had created a case of documents on me and my condition; they recorded how I smelled, my truck smelled, and my clothes smelled all while my peers were talking about me and expressing how they couldn't work around me. Many times, I would ask myself why I continued to put up with these conditions and put myself through these things day after day. Being by myself was the safest thing for me. Whenever I was alone in my truck, that's when I felt at ease. I would talk to myself. I would never beat myself up by saying mean and hurtful things to myself - I understood my condition. I didn't have to hide from myself. For so long, I figured that being alone was the best thing for me. I wanted a new life. Sadly, my reality wasn't going anywhere. Wherever I went, I took "me" and my condition along with me. From the age of twenty to the age of thirty-five, I felt like the same little boy who was sitting at my desk in the 2nd grade, watching the other kids in the room hold their noses while the teacher sprayed the room with air freshener. Because of my health, my time on that job had to come to an end. I knew it would one day happen; I just didn't know when.

You'd think that the process of having my disability benefits reinstated would be as easy as pie, but that's not the case. I was informed that by going to work, this made things harder. Social Security Disability denied me twice, which hurt because I am a person who was born disabled has never tried to play the system like some who're not legitimately disabled. Of course, this whole situation has been tough on my family; it has brought a lot of stress on my family and me. Whenever Satan is attacking our lives, he doesn't let up and hold back his attacks; it seems as if his attacks get worse before things get better. Out of nowhere, my wife started having seizures and blood clots in her lungs. I began to feel as if my world was falling apart. This experience was challenging my faith and my wife's faith to the fullest. All I ever wanted was the best for my family.

When you ask God to strengthen your faith, prepare for the ride of your life. I had to learn to trust God after not receiving a disability check for over a year. God kept my family and me. It was hard. I cried many nights. I worried many days, hours, minutes, and seconds. Few people came to the aide of my family and me. Going from being the sole provider in my household to not being able to provide tested me as a man, but it taught me to trust in God like never before. I felt like Daniel in the lion's den. The things that should have devoured me didn't. My faith never failed me even when the system, people, jobs, and many of my family and friends did. My heart remained faithful to the Lord. I did not know how God would provide for my family and me, but I knew that he would provide. This faith enables me to take pleasure in my weaknesses and endure the insults, hardships, persecution, and troubles that I encounter along the way, knowing that I do it all for Christ's sake. For when I am weak, God becomes my strength.

I asked Keiyawna one day, "If you knew the cost of being with me, would you still had chosen to pay the price?" She honestly answered,

"No way, Jack!"

Many people are faced with the question of "If they could do things all over again, would they do the same things they're doing?" Most people would do things differently if they had the chance to because the price is too high. After knowing what I know now, I would still choose my life and the route that I took (or the route that chose me). I always think about the fact that I have one of the rarest disabilities in the world - others who've had the same conditions and me have died because of these conditions. I'm one of the few people on the planet with my particular disabilities. I was never supposed to live pass childbirth. I was never supposed to have children. I thought I'd never get married - I mean, who would have wanted to marry a person like me? Sure, thinking back on my life, there are some things I probably should have never done: I should have never tried to work; I should have never played ball. But thank God my children are all healthy and very smart and talented. I teach people that no matter what their struggles, hurts, pains, and discomforts are, they shouldn't focus on the price of the journey - no one wants to pay the cost of suffering. But for me, things could have been much worse. The cost could be higher.

I believe that God still has much more for me to do and people to encourage and empower. I've come to the place in my life where I no longer try to make people like me and accept me. I know who and who can't put up with me and my condition. I don't stay in places that I'm not wanted. I've learned to treat people right, to not be mean the others, and not to hurt people because you never know what and why they're going through what they're going through. I've always felt bad for my brother Keith growing up. He'd always take up for me and take care of me. He never allowed people to pick on me. He'd still take a bullet for me today.

When alone, many times I feel saddened by the fact that many people who are around me don't know me. I know how people, regardless of race, gender, age, and religion, feels when mean and heartless people who don't understand them say mean and hurtful things to them. So what I try to teach people to do is not focus on people's disability, but rather, focus on their abilities; I try to teach them to love in spite of others' conditions.

If you're focused on making a difference in this life and this world, the price to pay will be high, but it is worth the cost. Allow God to catch people where they are. Clean people up where they are. Restore people back to where God has called them to be. There are many challenges that I face on a daily basis. I still have many struggles to overcome. But over the years, I've asked myself this one question: "If I stop doing what God has called me to do, then why should He continue to keep me alive?" I'm rooted and grounded in the reality that God has kept me alive for a reason.

I always encourage people to find a reason to live or to do whatever it is that they do; more importantly, I encourage them to discover what they've been created by God to do. I'm worth a billion dollars, not only because of Dr. Ricketts and his team who performed a miracle with the help of God but because I continue to fight to make an impact in this world every day with the many disabilities that I have. I have accepted the fact that I will never be like others. I've also accepted the fact that others will never be like me. Remember that you are a great gift from God. You must understand your worth. No one can devalue you. When you know your value, you'll understand that the pain and hurt that you feel doesn't compare to the value of the glory God is bestowing or getting ready to bestow on your life as a result of your condition. You're priceless. You can't put a price on your pains, your hurts, your struggles, and your disappointments; they are preparing you to make a mighty impact on the lives of countless others. Trust in the Lord and lean not on your own understanding. God will never allow you to suffer more than you can handle. You're being prepared by God for something great! Let God do what He intends to do in and through you. Your life is not your own; it belongs to God; it is His workmanship, His beautiful masterpiece which He is fashioning for His own purpose. Trust Him. Turn to Him. Bring your tears to Him and let Him heal and strengthen your heart today. Your journey lies ahead of you and your destination is...greatness. The greater the pain, the greater the glory.

About The Author

Calvin D. Ward is the oldest son of the late Willie Calvin Jones and Susanne Ward Henry. He began his ministry at the tender age of 12 years old. Calvin served faithfully under the leadership of the late Pastor Roy Hardin, Sr. in the Church of God in Christ for 27 years.

Calvin is a graduate of the Sure Foundation Theological Institute and he currently holds a Bachelor's degree. Calvin is currently working on his Master's degree in biblical studies.

Currently, Calvin Ward is the Senior Pastor of New Life at Hopkins Christian Church, which is an interdenominational ministry. Ordained as a bishop, many regard Bishop Calvin Ward as a powerful, anointed preacher and teacher of the Word of God, and a walking miracle.

Calvin resides in Atlanta, Georgia with his wife Keiyawna. They are the proud parents of three beautiful daughters: Kahleighya, Kemia, and Kaela. Calvin's passion in life is to love the lost, forgive the forgotten, and restore the restless.

To contact the author, go to:
Calvinward2002@yahoo.com
www.NewLifeAtHopkins.com
Facebook: Bishop Calvin D. Ward
Facebook: Newlifeathopkins

CPSIA information can be obtained
at www.ICGtesting.com
Printed in the USA
FSHW04n1044110418
46582FS